Rebecca Bates

Daily Devotional For Black Women 2023

A 30-Day Devotional with Bible Scriptures and Activities for Connecting with God, Cultivating Faith, and Overcoming Anxiety in 2023

Copyright © 2023 by Rebecca Bates

All rights reserved. No part of this publication may be reproduced, stored or transmitted in any form or by any means, electronic, mechanical, photocopying, recording, scanning, or otherwise without written permission from the publisher. It is illegal to copy this book, post it to a website, or distribute it by any other means without permission.

First edition

This book was professionally typeset on Reedsy
Find out more at reedsy.com

"You are altogether beautiful, my darling, beautiful in every way."

- Song of Songs 4:7

Contents

I. Introduction: 1
How to use this daily devotional 1
II. Daily Devotions 5
Day 1: Overcoming Adversity and Embracing Resilience 5
Day 2: Cultivating Self-Care and Self-Love 5
Day 3: Trusting in God's plan and finding peace in uncertainty 5
Day 4: Embracing and celebrating our cultural heritage and identity 5
Day 5: Navigating Interpersonal relationships and building community 5
Day 6: Reflecting on personal growth and gratitude 5
Day 7: Finding strength in our faith and spirituality 5
Day 8: Understanding and Healing from Trauma 5
Day 9: Forgiveness and Letting go 5
Day 10: Empowerment and Leadership 5
Day 11: Self-Discovery and Purpose 5
Day 12: Overcoming negative self-talk and affirming oneself 5
Day 13: Building and sustaining healthy relationships 5
Day 14: Practicing gratitude and mindfulness 5
Day 15: Understanding and managing stress and anxiety 5
Day 16: Embracing our uniqueness and individuality 5
Day 17: Nurturing and protecting mental and emotional well-being . 5
Day 18: Learning to set boundaries and assert oneself 5
Day 19: Building a support system and community 5
Day 20: Celebrating and honoring our ancestors and heritage 5

Day 21: Trusting the journey and embracing change...................5
Day 22: Finding beauty and joy in the present moment..................5
Day 23: Overcoming obstacles and achieving goals 5
Day 24: Cultivating positive self-image and self-worth....................5
Day 25: Understanding and practicing self-compassion 5
Day 26: Embracing and learning from failure....................................5
Day 27: Understanding and practicing forgiveness...........................5
Day 28: Cultivating inner peace and tranquility................................5
Day 29: Reflecting on personal growth and progress........................5
Day 30: Embracing Hope and Looking Forward to the Future..........5
III. Additional Resources..46
IV. Conclusion..48

1.
   1.
2.
   1.
   2.
   3.
   4.
   5.
   6.
   7.
   8.
   9.
   10.
   11.

12.
13.
14.
15.
16.
17.
18.
19.
20.
21.
22.
23.
24.
25.
26.
27.
28.
29.
30.

3.

Hero Adeleke
Tyrran Lewis

I. Introduction:

As a Black Christian woman, I understand the unique challenges and experiences that come with being a Black woman in today's society. From navigating systemic racism to finding representation and understanding in our faith communities, the journey toward self-discovery, acceptance, and empowerment can be a difficult one. This is why I have created this daily devotional, specifically for Black women, to provide daily encouragement, guidance, and inspiration as we navigate our lives and our relationship with God.

The daily devotions in this book focus on themes such as self-care, self-love, cultural identity, and resilience, to help Black women find strength, peace, and purpose in their lives. Each day's devotion will center around a different theme and will include Bible verses, personal reflections, and practical tips for putting the lessons into practice in daily life.

As a Black woman, I have faced many struggles in my journey toward self-discovery, acceptance, and empowerment, but through my relationship with God, I have found the strength and guidance I need to navigate the challenges I face. This devotional is a reflection of my journey, and I hope it will serve as a guide for other Black women as they navigate their own.

One of the most important lessons I have learned is that growing closer to God as a Black woman requires a unique approach. It requires acknowledging and embracing our cultural heritage, understanding the unique experiences we face as Black women, and finding representation and understanding within our faith communities. I have found that by doing so, I have been able to build a deeper and more meaningful relationship with God.

Throughout this devotional, I will share my own story and experiences, as well as the lessons I have learned on my journey toward self-discovery, acceptance, and empowerment. I hope that by sharing my story, other Black women will be inspired to embark on their journey toward a deeper and more meaningful relationship with God.

The daily devotions in this book are designed to be a resource for Black women as they navigate their lives and their relationship with God. By reading and reflecting on the daily devotions, Black women will find the encouragement, guidance, and inspiration they need to build a deeper and more meaningful relationship with God.

So, join me on this journey of self-discovery, acceptance, and empowerment, as we navigate the unique challenges and experiences of being a Black woman in today's society, and work towards building a deeper and more meaningful relationship with God.

This devotional is for Black women who are looking for a deeper connection with God and want to navigate their unique challenges and experiences with the help of their faith. It will provide daily inspiration, guidance, and encouragement as we navigate life's challenges and build a meaningful relationship with God.

How to use this daily devotional

To get the most out of this daily devotional, it is recommended to set aside some time each day to read and reflect on the daily devotion. Some suggestions for when to read the devotions include first thing in the morning as a way to start the day with inspiration and guidance, or at night as a way to reflect on the day and gain a sense of peace and closure.

When reading the daily devotion, take your time to read through the Bible verse and personal reflections provided. Reflect on the theme of the day and think about how it relates to your own life and experiences. Take note of any insights or revelations that come to mind, and consider how you can apply the lessons from the devotion to your own life.

In addition to reading and reflecting on the daily devotion, it may be helpful to incorporate other practices into your daily routine such as prayer, journaling, or meditating. These practices can help to deepen your connection with God and provide additional support as you navigate the challenges and experiences of your daily life.

It's also important to keep in mind that this devotional is not a one-time read, but rather a daily companion that will provide ongoing support and guidance as you continue on your journey of self-discovery, acceptance, and empowerment. It's not about perfection or reading it every day, but about making an effort to incorporate it into your daily routine and finding what works best for you.

Finally, don't hesitate to reach out to others, whether friends, family, or members of your faith community, for support and guidance. Building a support system and community can be an invaluable resource as you navigate the unique challenges and experiences of being a Black woman in today's society.

II. Daily Devotions

Day 1: Overcoming Adversity and Embracing Resilience

Bible Verse: *"I can do all things through Christ who strengthens me."* - Philippians 4:13

Reflection: As Black women, we often face adversity and challenges in our lives. From navigating systemic racism to dealing with personal struggles, it can be easy to feel overwhelmed and defeated. However, as believers in Christ, we have the strength and resilience to overcome any obstacle that comes our way.

The Bible verse for today reminds us that through Christ, we have the strength to overcome any adversity and challenge that comes our way. This strength doesn't come from within us, but from the power of Christ working within us.

As we face adversity and challenges, it's important to remember that we are not alone. Christ is with us every step of the way, providing us with the strength and resilience we need to overcome any obstacle.

Practice: Take a moment to reflect on the challenges and obstacles you are currently facing. Ask God to give you the strength and resilience you need to overcome them. Then, take a step of faith and trust that, with God's help, you can overcome any adversity that comes your way.

Prayer: Dear Lord, we come to you today with heavy hearts, feeling overwhelmed by the challenges and obstacles we face. We ask that you give us the strength and resilience we need to overcome them. We trust that through you, all things are possible. Help us to take a step of faith and trust that, with your help, we can overcome any adversity that comes our way. Amen.

Affirmation: I am strong, I am resilient, and I can overcome any obstacle that comes my way through the strength of Christ.

Day 2: Cultivating Self-Care and Self-Love

Bible Verse: *"Love your neighbor as yourself."* - Matthew 22:39

Reflection: As Black women, we often put the needs of others before our own, neglecting our self-care and self-love in the process. However, as believers in Christ, we are called to love and care for ourselves just as we would love and care for our neighbors. Self-care and self-love are not selfish acts, but rather necessary components of leading a healthy and fulfilling life.

The Bible verse for today reminds us that we are called to love ourselves just as we would love our neighbors. By taking care of ourselves physically, emotionally, and spiritually, we are better able to love and serve others.

Practice: Take some time today to reflect on how you currently practice self-care and self-love. Identify areas in which you can improve and make a plan to incorporate more self-care and self-love into your daily routine.

Prayer: Dear Lord, we come to you today to recognize the importance of self-care and self-love in leading a healthy and fulfilling life. We ask for your guidance as we strive to love ourselves just as we would love our neighbors. Help us to make self-care and self-love a priority in our lives, so that we may be better able to love and serve others. Amen.

Affirmation: I am worthy of love and care, and I choose to prioritize self-care and self-love in my daily life.

Day 3: Trusting in God's plan and finding peace in uncertainty

Bible Verse: *"Trust in the Lord with all your heart, and lean not on your understanding; In all your ways acknowledge Him, and He shall direct your paths."* - Proverbs 3:5-6

Reflection: It can be easy to get caught up in worrying about the future and the uncertainty of life. As Black women, we may have additional uncertainty and fears due to the systemic issues we face. However, as believers in Christ, we are called to trust in God's plan for our lives and to find peace amid uncertainty.

The Bible verse for today reminds us that by trusting in the Lord with all of our hearts and acknowledging Him in all of our ways, He will direct our paths and guide us through any uncertainty.

Practice: Take a moment to reflect on any areas of uncertainty in your life. Bring these worries and fears to God in prayer and ask for His guidance and direction. Trust in His plan for your life and find peace in the uncertainty.

Prayer: Dear Lord, we come to you today with heavy hearts, feeling overwhelmed by the uncertainty of the future. We ask that you guide us and direct our paths. Help us to trust in your plan for our lives, and find peace amid uncertainty. Amen.

Affirmation: I trust in God's plan for my life, and find peace amid uncertainty.

Day 4: Embracing and celebrating our cultural heritage and identity

Bible Verse: *"For we are God's handiwork, created in Christ Jesus to do good works, which God prepared in advance for us to do."* - Ephesians 2:10

Reflection: As Black women, our cultural heritage and identity play a significant role in shaping who we are and how we navigate the world. However, due to societal and systemic issues, it can be easy to feel like our cultural heritage and identity are not valued or respected. As believers in Christ, we are reminded that we are uniquely created by God and have been called to do good works, which includes embracing and celebrating our cultural heritage and identity.

The Bible verse for today reminds us that we are God's handiwork, created with a purpose and for a specific reason. We should embrace and celebrate our cultural heritage and identity as it is a unique part of who we are and how God has created us.

Practice: Take some time today to reflect on your cultural heritage and identity. Consider how it has shaped who you are and how you navigate the world. Celebrate the beauty and richness of your cultural heritage and identity.

Prayer: Dear Lord, we come to you today grateful for the unique cultural heritage and identity you have given us. We ask for your guidance as we embrace and celebrate the beauty and richness of who we are. Help us to see the value and worth of our cultural heritage and identity, and give us the courage to share it with others. Give us the wisdom and discernment to navigate any challenges or obstacles that may arise as we celebrate our cultural heritage and identity. We trust in your plan for our lives and ask for your continued guidance as we journey through this world, Amen.

Affirmation: I embrace and celebrate my cultural heritage and identity, recognizing the value and worth it brings to who I am as a person, and I am proud of my cultural heritage and identity.

Day 5: Navigating Interpersonal relationships and building community

Bible Verse: *"Two are better than one because they have a good return for their labor: If either of them falls, one can help the other up. But pity anyone who falls and has no one to help them up."* - Ecclesiastes 4:9-10

Reflection: As Black women, navigating interpersonal relationships can be challenging. From dealing with stereotypes and biases to building a sense of community and belonging, it can be difficult to find the support and understanding we need. However, as believers in Christ, we are called to build strong and supportive relationships with others, recognizing that in the community, we find strength and the ability to help one another in times of need.

The Bible verse for today reminds us that two are better than one and that in a community, we find strength and the ability to help one another in times of need. We need to surround ourselves with people who will support and uplift us.

Practice: Take some time today to reflect on the relationships in your life. Consider how they are supportive and uplifting, and identify areas where you could benefit from building stronger relationships. Make a plan to build community and surround yourself with people who will support and uplift you.

Prayer: Dear Lord, we come to you today to recognize the importance of strong and supportive relationships in our lives. We ask for your guidance as we navigate interpersonal relationships and build community. Help us to surround ourselves with people who will support and uplift us, and give us the wisdom and discernment to navigate any challenges or obstacles that may arise in our relationships. Amen.

Affirmation: I am surrounded by strong and supportive relationships that uplift and empower me.

Day 6: Reflecting on personal growth and gratitude

Bible Verse: *"Give thanks in all circumstances; for this is God's will for you in Christ Jesus."* - 1 Thessalonians 5:18

Reflection: As Black women, we often focus on the challenges and obstacles in our lives, neglecting to take the time to reflect on the progress and growth we have made. However, as believers in Christ, it is important to take a step back and reflect on our personal growth and practice gratitude for the blessings in our lives.

The Bible verse for today reminds us to give thanks in all circumstances, recognizing that gratitude is God's will for us in Christ Jesus. By taking the time to reflect on our personal growth and practice gratitude, we can see the blessings in our lives and have a more positive outlook on our journey.

Practice: Take some time today to reflect on the progress and growth you have made in your life. Make a list of the things you are grateful for and take note of the blessings in your life. Practice gratitude by expressing thankfulness for the things in your life, both big and small.

Prayer: Dear Lord, we come to you today grateful for the progress and growth we have made in our lives. We ask for your guidance as we reflect on our journey and practice gratitude for the blessings in our lives. Help us to see the beauty and positivity in our lives and to have a more positive outlook on our journey. Amen.

Affirmation: I am grateful for the progress and growth I have made in my life and I am blessed with many things to be thankful for.

Day 7: Finding strength in our faith and spirituality

Bible Verse: "But those who hope in the Lord will renew their strength. They will soar on wings like eagles; they will run and not grow weary, they will walk and not be faint." - Isaiah 40:31

Reflection: As Black women, we may face challenges and obstacles that test our faith and spirituality. However, as believers in Christ, we are reminded that our hope and strength come from the Lord. By placing our trust in Him and cultivating a strong spiritual foundation, we can find the strength and resilience we need to navigate life's challenges.

The Bible verse for today reminds us that those who hope in the Lord will renew their strength. By placing our trust in God and cultivating a strong spiritual foundation, we will be able to soar above our challenges, run without growing weary and walk without fainting.

Practice: Take some time today to reflect on your faith and spirituality. Consider how you currently cultivate a strong spiritual foundation and identify areas where you could benefit from further growth. Make a plan to strengthen your faith and spirituality by incorporating practices such as prayer, reading scripture, and attending church or fellowship.

Prayer: Dear Lord, we come to you today to recognize the importance of our faith and spirituality in navigating life's challenges. We ask for your guidance as we strive to cultivate a strong spiritual foundation and place our trust in you. Help us to find strength and resilience in our faith and to soar above any obstacles that come our way. Amen.

Affirmation: I find strength and resilience in my faith and spirituality, and I trust in the Lord to guide me through life's challenges.

Day 8: Understanding and Healing from Trauma

Bible Verse: *"He heals the brokenhearted and binds up their wounds."* - Psalm 147:3

Reflection: As Black women, we may have experienced trauma due to systemic issues and racism. Trauma can have a profound effect on our mental, emotional and physical well-being. However, as believers in Christ, we are reminded that God is a healer and that He can heal the brokenhearted and bind up their wounds.

The Bible verse for today reminds us that God is a compassionate and loving God who has the power to heal our trauma and bring peace and healing to our lives. It's important for us to acknowledge and process our trauma, and to trust in God's healing power.

Practice: Take some time today to reflect on any trauma you have experienced. Acknowledge the trauma and its effect on your life. Pray and ask God to bring healing and peace to your mind, body, and soul. If you need professional help, don't hesitate to seek it out.

Prayer: Dear Lord, we come to you today to acknowledge the trauma we have experienced in our lives. We ask for your healing and peace to mend our broken hearts and bind up our wounds. Help us to trust in our power to heal and to have the strength to seek out the help we need to work through our trauma. We trust in your love and compassion, Amen.

Affirmation: I trust in God's power to heal and I am on a path toward peace and healing from my trauma.

Day 9: Forgiveness and Letting go

Bible Verse: *"For if you forgive other people when they sin against you, your heavenly Father will also forgive you. But if you do not forgive others their sins, your Father will not forgive your sins."* - Matthew 6:14-15

Reflection: As Black women, we may have experienced hurt and pain from others, whether it be from personal relationships or from the systemic issues and racism we face. Holding on to these grudges and resentments can weigh heavy on our hearts and prevent us from moving forward. However, as believers in Christ, we are called to forgive and let go of these feelings to find peace and healing.

The Bible verse for today reminds us that forgiveness is not only important for the well-being of others, but for our well-being as well.

By forgiving and letting go, we open ourselves up to the forgiveness and healing that God offers.

Practice: Take some time today to reflect on any hurt or pain you may be holding onto from others. Consider how forgiveness and letting go can bring peace and healing to your heart. Make a plan to practice forgiveness, whether it be through prayer, therapy, or other means.

Prayer: Dear Lord, we come to you today acknowledging the hurt and pain we have experienced from others. We ask for your guidance and strength as we work towards forgiveness and letting go. Help us to see the value in forgiveness not only for the well-being of others but for our well-being as well. We trust in your love and compassion, Amen.

Affirmation: I choose to forgive and let go of past hurt and pain, finding peace and healing through the power of forgiveness.

Day 10: Empowerment and Leadership

Bible Verse: *"She is clothed with strength and dignity, and she laughs without fear of the future."* - Proverbs 31:25

Reflection: As Black women, we may face challenges and obstacles in asserting ourselves as leaders and feeling empowered in our own lives. However, as believers in Christ, we are reminded that we are strong and capable individuals, created to lead and make a difference in the world.

The Bible verse for today reminds us that when we have strength and dignity, we can face the future with confidence and joy. We need to embrace our power and take on leadership roles in our personal and professional lives.

Practice: Take some time today to reflect on your sense of empowerment and leadership. Consider how you currently assert yourself as a leader and identify areas where you could benefit from further development. Make a plan to empower yourself and assert yourself as a leader by setting goals, taking on new challenges, and seeking out mentorship or leadership training.

Prayer: Dear Lord, we come to you today seeking strength, dignity, and the courage to lead. We ask for your guidance as we strive to empower ourselves and assert ourselves as leaders in our personal and professional lives. Help us to see the value in our leadership abilities and to make a positive difference in the world. Amen.

Affirmation: I am strong, capable, and a leader, I embrace my power and make a positive difference in the world.

Day 11: Self-Discovery and Purpose

Bible Verse: *"For I know the plans I have for you, declares the Lord, plans to prosper you and not to harm you, plans to give you hope and a future."* - Jeremiah 29:11

Reflection: As Black women, we may struggle with finding our purpose and understanding our unique place in the world. However, as believers in Christ, we are reminded that God has a plan for our lives and that He has created us with a unique purpose and destiny.

The Bible verse for today reminds us that God has a plan for our lives and that it includes prosperity, hope, and a future. We need to take the time to discover our purpose, and to trust in God's plan for our lives.

Practice: Take some time today to reflect on your sense of purpose and destiny. Consider the things that bring you passion and fulfillment, and ask God to reveal your purpose to you. Make a plan to explore your passions and talents, and seek out opportunities that align with your purpose.

Prayer: Dear Lord, we come to you today seeking an understanding of our purpose and place in the world. We ask for your guidance as we strive for self-discovery and to understand the plans you have for our lives. Help us to trust in your plan for us and to find fulfillment and meaning in the path you have set before us. Amen.

Affirmation: I trust in God's plan for my life and I am constantly discovering my purpose and fulfilling my destiny.

Day 12: Overcoming negative self-talk and affirming oneself

Bible Verse: *"So God created mankind in his own image, in the image of God he created them; male and female he created them."* - Genesis 1:27

Reflection: As Black women, we may struggle with negative self-talk and a lack of self-confidence. However, as believers in Christ, we are reminded that we are created in the image of God and therefore have inherent worth and value.

The Bible verse for today reminds us that we are created in the image of God and therefore have inherent worth and value. It's important for us to overcome negative self-talk and to affirm ourselves, recognizing the unique and valuable contributions we make to the world.

Practice: Take some time today to reflect on your own negative self-talk. Identify the specific thoughts and beliefs that hold you back and challenge them with positive affirmations. Make a plan to regularly remind yourself of your worth and value, and to speak kindly and positively to yourself.

Prayer: Dear Lord, we come to you today acknowledging the negative thoughts and beliefs that hold us back. We ask for your guidance and strength as we work to overcome these thoughts and affirm ourselves. Help us to see ourselves as you see us, created in your image with inherent worth and value. Amen.

Affirmation: I am created in the image of God, and therefore I have inherent worth and value. I choose to overcome negative self-talk and affirm myself.

Day 13: Building and sustaining healthy relationships

Bible Verse: *"Love is patient, love is kind. It does not envy, it does not boast, it is not proud. It does not dishonor others, it is not self-seeking, it is not easily angered, it keeps no record of wrongs."* - 1 Corinthians 13:4-5

Reflection: As Black women, we may struggle with building and sustaining healthy relationships. However, as believers in Christ, we are called to love others, including ourselves, with patience, kindness, and selflessness.

The Bible verse for today reminds us of the characteristics of true love and how it should be expressed in our relationships. We need to build and sustain healthy relationships based on these principles.

Practice: Take some time today to reflect on the relationships in your life. Consider how they align with the characteristics of love described in 1 Corinthians 13:4-5. Make a plan to actively work on building and sustaining healthy relationships, whether it be through effective communication, setting boundaries, or forgiveness.

Prayer: Dear Lord, we come to you today to recognize the importance of healthy relationships in our lives. We ask for your guidance as we work to build and sustain relationships based on love, patience, kindness, and selflessness. Help us to love ourselves and others with your love, Amen.

Affirmation: I choose to build and sustain healthy relationships based on love, patience, kindness, and selflessness.

Day 14: Practicing gratitude and mindfulness

Bible Verse: *"Be thankful in all circumstances, for this is God's will for you who belong to Christ Jesus."* - 1 Thessalonians 5:18

Reflection: As Black women, we may struggle with feeling overwhelmed and anxious in our daily lives. However, as believers in Christ, we are reminded to practice gratitude and mindfulness to find peace and contentment in our circumstances.

The Bible verse for today reminds us to be thankful in all circumstances, as it is God's will for us. We need to take the time to focus on the present moment and to be thankful for the blessings in our lives.

Practice: Take some time today to practice mindfulness and gratitude. Make a list of things you are thankful for and take note of the blessings in your life. Take a few minutes to be present in the moment and focus on your breathing. Make it a habit to practice gratitude and mindfulness regularly.

Prayer: Dear Lord, we come to you today seeking peace and contentment in our daily lives. We ask for your guidance as we practice gratitude and mindfulness. Help us to focus on the present moment and to be thankful for the blessings in our lives. Amen.

Affirmation: I choose to practice gratitude and mindfulness, finding peace and contentment in the present moment.

Day 15: Understanding and managing stress and anxiety

Bible Verse: *"Cast all your anxiety on him because he cares for you."* - 1 Peter 5:7

Reflection: As Black women, we may struggle with managing stress and anxiety in our daily lives, due to systemic issues and racism. However, as believers in Christ, we are reminded that we can cast all our anxieties on God, as He cares for us.

The Bible verse for today reminds us that we can trust in God's care for us and that He can help us manage our stress and anxiety. It's important for us to understand the sources of our stress and anxiety and to develop healthy coping mechanisms.

Practice: Take some time today to reflect on your own stress and anxiety. Identify the sources and triggers of your stress and anxiety, and develop a plan to manage them. Incorporate healthy coping mechanisms such as exercise, mindfulness, and prayer. Remember to rely on God's care and guidance in managing stress and anxiety.

Prayer: Dear Lord, we come to you today acknowledging the stress and anxiety we feel in our daily lives. We ask for your guidance and support as we work to understand and manage these feelings. We cast all our anxieties on you, trusting in your care for us. Amen.

Affirmation: I trust in God's care for me and I am equipped with the skills and resources to manage my stress and anxiety.

Day 16: Embracing our uniqueness and individuality

Bible Verse: *"For we are God's handiwork, created in Christ Jesus to do good works, which God prepared in advance for us to do."* - Ephesians 2:10

Reflection: As Black women, we may struggle with feeling pressure to conform to societal expectations and standards. However, as believers in Christ, we are reminded that we are uniquely created by God and have a purpose and individuality that should be embraced.

The Bible verse for today reminds us that we are God's handiwork, created with a purpose and individuality that should be honored and celebrated. We need to embrace our uniqueness and not be afraid to be ourselves.

Practice: Take some time today to reflect on your own individuality and uniqueness. Consider the things that make you unique and special and make a plan to honor and celebrate them. Remind yourself that you are fearfully and wonderfully made and that your individuality is a gift from God.

Prayer: Dear Lord, we come to you today to acknowledge the pressure to conform to societal expectations. We ask for your guidance as we work to embrace our individuality and uniqueness. Help us to see ourselves as you see us, fearfully and wonderfully made, with a purpose and individuality that should be honored and celebrated. Amen.

Affirmation: I am uniquely and wonderfully made by God, and I embrace my individuality and uniqueness.

Day 17: Nurturing and protecting mental and emotional well-being

Bible Verse: *"He himself bore our sins in his body on the cross, so that we might die to sins and live for righteousness; by his wounds, you have been healed."* - 1 Peter 2:24

Reflection: As Black women, we may struggle with maintaining positive mental and emotional well-being due to systemic issues and racism. However, as believers in Christ, we are reminded that through His sacrifice on the cross, we have been healed.

The Bible verse for today reminds us that through Jesus' sacrifice, we have been forgiven and healed. It's important for us to nurture and protect our mental and emotional well-being by seeking forgiveness and healing through Jesus, and to also take care of ourselves through self-care and seeking help when needed.

Practice: Take some time today to reflect on your own mental and emotional well-being. Consider the things that contribute to your well-being and make a plan to take care of yourself. Make sure to seek forgiveness and healing through Jesus and to also seek help when needed, whether it be through therapy or other professional help.

Prayer: Dear Lord, we come to you today to acknowledge the struggles we face in maintaining positive mental and emotional well-being. We ask for your guidance and healing as we work to take care of ourselves. We trust in your sacrifice on the cross and the healing and forgiveness it brings. Amen.

Affirmation: I trust in the healing and forgiveness found in Jesus and I commit to nurturing and protecting my mental and emotional well-being.

Day 18: Learning to set boundaries and assert oneself

Bible Verse: *"Therefore, as God's chosen people, holy and dearly loved, clothe yourselves with compassion, kindness, humility, gentleness, and patience."* - Colossians 3:12

Reflection: As Black women, we may struggle with setting boundaries and asserting ourselves in our personal and professional lives. However, as believers in Christ, we are called to clothe ourselves with compassion, kindness, humility, gentleness, and patience.

The Bible verse for today reminds us that as God's chosen people, we are called to embody these virtues in our interactions with others, which includes setting boundaries and asserting ourselves. We need to learn how to communicate our needs and wants effectively, while also showing compassion and kindness to others.

Practice: Take some time today to reflect on your own boundaries and how they are being respected. Consider how you currently assert yourself and identify areas where you could benefit from further development. Make a plan to communicate your needs and wants effectively, while also showing compassion and kindness to others.

Prayer: Dear Lord, we come to you today seeking guidance in setting boundaries and asserting ourselves. We ask for your help in communicating our needs and wants effectively, while also showing compassion and kindness to others. Help us to embody the virtues of compassion, kindness, humility, gentleness, and patience in all our interactions. Amen.

Affirmation: I choose to communicate my needs and wants effectively, while also showing compassion and kindness to others. I am learning to set boundaries and assert myself.

Day 19: Building a support system and community

Bible Verse: *"And let us consider how we may spur one another on toward love and good deeds, not giving up meeting together, as some are in the habit of doing, but encouraging one another—and all the more as you see the Day approaching."* - Hebrews 10:24-25

Reflection: As Black women, we may struggle with feeling alone and unsupported, especially in the face of systemic issues and racism. However, as believers in Christ, we are called to build a support system and community by encouraging one another and coming together to love and do good deeds.

The Bible verse for today reminds us of the importance of coming together and encouraging one another. We need to build a support system and community, whether it be through church, community groups, or friendships, to have a source of love, support, and encouragement.

Practice: Take some time today to reflect on your own support system and community. Consider how you currently connect with others and identify areas where you could benefit from further support. Make a plan to build a support system and community, whether it be through joining a group or reaching out to friends or family for support.

Prayer: Dear Lord, we come to you today to recognize the importance of having a support system and community. We ask for your guidance as we work to build a community of love, support, and encouragement. Help us to come together and spur one another on towards love and good deeds. Amen.

Affirmation: I am building a support system and community, where I find love, support, and encouragement.

Day 20: Celebrating and honoring our ancestors and heritage

Bible Verse: *"The Lord is my strength and my shield; in him my heart trusts, and I am helped; my heart exults, and with my song, I give thanks to him."* - Psalm 28:7

Reflection: As Black women, we need to honor and celebrate our ancestors and heritage, as it is a fundamental part of our identity. We should be proud of our history and culture, and the sacrifices and struggles of our ancestors, while acknowledging the systemic issues that have affected and continue to affect our communities. By celebrating and honoring our heritage, we can connect with our past and find strength and resilience in the face of adversity.

The Bible verse for today reminds us that the Lord is our strength and shield, and we can trust in Him to guide us through the journey of celebrating and honoring our ancestors and heritage. It's important for us to trust in God and to give thanks to Him, as we honor and celebrate our ancestors and heritage.

Practice: Take some time today to reflect on your own ancestors and heritage. Learn about your family history and the sacrifices and struggles of your ancestors. Connect with your culture and community, whether it be through food, music, or language. Make a plan to celebrate and honor your ancestors and heritage regularly.

Prayer: Dear Lord, we come to you today to recognize the importance of honoring and celebrating our ancestors and heritage. We ask for your guidance as we work to connect with our past and find strength and resilience in the face of adversity. We trust in you and give thanks for the sacrifices and struggles of our ancestors. Amen.

Affirmation: I celebrate and honor my ancestors and heritage, connecting with my past and finding strength and resilience in the face of adversity.

Day 21: Trusting the journey and embracing change

Bible Verse: *"I know the plans I have for you,"* declares the Lord, *"plans to prosper you and not to harm you, plans to give you hope and a future."* - Jeremiah 29:11

Reflection: As Black women, we may struggle with uncertainty and change in our lives. However, as believers in Christ, we are reminded that God has a plan for us and that His plans are for our prosperity and future.

The Bible verse for today reminds us that God has a plan for us and that we can trust in Him to guide us through the journey of life, even in times of change and uncertainty. It's important for us to trust in

God's plan and to embrace change, knowing that He is in control and will bring about good for us.

Practice: Take some time today to reflect on the changes and uncertainties in your life. Remind yourself that God has a plan for you and that He will bring about good for you. Make a plan to trust in God's plan and to embrace change, whether it be through prayer, journaling, or seeking guidance from a mentor or counselor.

Prayer: Dear Lord, we come to you today acknowledging the uncertainty and change in our lives. We ask for your guidance and wisdom as we work to trust in your plan and embrace change. We trust in your promise to prosper us and to give us hope and a future. Amen.

Affirmation: I trust in God's plan for my life and embrace change, knowing that He is in control and will bring about good for me.

Day 22: Finding beauty and joy in the present moment

Bible Verse: *"This is the day the Lord has made; let us rejoice and be glad in it."* - Psalm 118:24

Reflection: As Black women, we may struggle with finding joy and beauty in the present moment due to the stress and challenges of daily life. However, as believers in Christ, we are reminded to find joy in the present moment and to give thanks to God for the blessings in our lives.

The Bible verse for today reminds us that each day is a gift from God and that we should rejoice and be glad in it. We need to take the time to appreciate the present moment and to find joy in the small things in life.

Practice: Take some time today to focus on the present moment. Take notice of the beauty around you, whether it be the colors of nature, the sound of birds singing, or the smell of a fresh breeze. Make a plan to find joy in the present moment, whether it be through gratitude journaling, mindfulness, or spending time with loved ones.

Prayer: Dear Lord, we come to you today seeking guidance in finding joy and beauty in the present moment. We ask for your help in appreciating the small things in life and giving thanks for the blessings in our lives. We trust in your promise that this is the day you have made, and we will rejoice and be glad in it. Amen.

Affirmation: I find joy and beauty in the present moment, and I give thanks to God for the blessings in my life.

Day 23: Overcoming obstacles and achieving goals

Bible Verse: *"I can do all things through him who strengthens me."*
- Philippians 4:13

Reflection: As Black women, we may struggle with overcoming obstacles and achieving our goals due to systemic issues and racism. However, as believers in Christ, we are reminded that through His strength and guidance, we can overcome any obstacle and achieve our goals.

The Bible verse for today reminds us that we can do all things through Christ who strengthens us. We need to trust in God's strength and guidance as we work towards overcoming obstacles and achieving our goals.

Practice: Take some time today to reflect on the obstacles and goals in your life. Make a plan to overcome those obstacles and achieve those goals, whether it be through setting realistic steps, seeking guidance or support, and reminding yourself of God's strength and guidance.

Prayer: Dear Lord, we come to you today seeking your strength and guidance as we work towards overcoming obstacles and achieving our goals. We trust in your promise that through you, we can do all things. We ask for your help in setting realistic steps, seeking guidance and support, and reminding ourselves of your strength and guidance. Amen.

Affirmation: I trust in God's strength and guidance as I work towards overcoming obstacles and achieving my goals.

Day 24: Cultivating positive self-image and self-worth

Bible Verse: *"So God created man in his own image, in the image of God he created him; male and female he created them."* - Genesis 1:27

Reflection: As Black women, we may struggle with negative self-image and self-worth due to societal pressures and racism. However, as believers in Christ, we are reminded that we are made in the image of God and have inherent value and worth.

The Bible verse for today reminds us that we are created in the image of God and that we have inherent value and worth. It's important for us to remind ourselves of this truth and to cultivate a positive self-image and self-worth by focusing on our strengths and abilities, and by valuing ourselves as God values us.

Practice: Take some time today to reflect on your own self-image and self-worth. Make a list of your strengths and abilities. Remind yourself of your inherent value and worth as a child of God. Make a plan to focus on your strengths and abilities, and to value yourself as God values you.

Prayer: Dear Lord, we come to you today to acknowledge the struggles we face in cultivating positive self-image and self-worth. We ask for your guidance as we work to focus on our strengths and abilities and to value ourselves as you value us. Help us to remember that we are made in your image and have inherent value and worth. Amen.

Affirmation: I am made in the image of God and have inherent value and worth. I focus on my strengths and abilities, and I value myself as God values me.

Day 25: Understanding and practicing self-compassion

Bible Verse: *"Therefore, as God's chosen people, holy and dearly loved, clothe yourselves with compassion, kindness, humility, gentleness, and patience."* - Colossians 3:12

Reflection: As Black women, we may struggle with self-compassion due to societal expectations and racism. However, as believers in Christ, we are reminded to clothe ourselves with compassion, kindness, humility, gentleness, and patience, including towards ourselves.

The Bible verse for today reminds us that as God's chosen people, we are called to embody these virtues in our interactions with ourselves and others. We need to practice self-compassion by being kind and understanding towards ourselves, forgiving ourselves when we make mistakes, and treating ourselves with the same compassion and understanding that we would offer to a friend.

Practice: Take some time today to reflect on how you treat yourself. Consider how you talk to yourself and how you respond to your mistakes. Make a plan to practice self-compassion by being kind and understanding towards yourself, forgiving yourself when you make mistakes, and treating yourself with the same compassion and understanding that you would offer to a friend.

Prayer: Dear Lord, we come to you today seeking guidance in practicing self-compassion. We ask for your help in being kind and understanding towards ourselves, forgiving ourselves when we make mistakes, and treating ourselves with the same compassion and understanding that we would offer to a friend. Help us to embody the virtues of compassion, kindness, humility, gentleness, and patience in our interactions with ourselves and others. Amen.

Affirmation: I practice self-compassion by being kind and understanding towards myself, forgiving myself when I make mistakes, and treating myself with the same compassion and understanding that I would offer to a friend.

Day 26: Embracing and learning from failure

Bible Verse: *"Therefore, my dear brothers and sisters, stand firm. Let nothing move you. Always give yourselves fully to the work of the Lord, because you know that your labor in the Lord is not in vain."* - 1 Corinthians 15:58

Reflection: As Black women, we may struggle with embracing and learning from failure due to societal expectations and racism. However, as believers in Christ, we are reminded that our labor in the Lord is not in vain, and that failure is an opportunity for growth and learning.

The Bible verse for today reminds us that we should stand firm in our faith and give ourselves fully to the work of the Lord, knowing that our efforts are not in vain. It's important for us to embrace failure as an opportunity for growth and learning, and to trust in God's plan for our lives.

Practice: Take some time today to reflect on past failures and how you responded to them. Make a plan to embrace failure as an opportunity for growth and learning, whether it be through seeking feedback, learning from your mistakes, or finding a mentor or coach.

Prayer: Dear Lord, we come to you today to acknowledge the struggles we face in embracing and learning from failure. We ask for your guidance as we work to see failure as an opportunity for growth and learning. We trust in your plan for our lives and give ourselves fully to the work of the Lord, knowing that our efforts are not in vain. Amen.

Affirmation: I embrace failure as an opportunity for growth and learning, and I trust in God's plan for my life.

Day 27: Understanding and practicing forgiveness

Bible Verse: *"Be kind and compassionate to one another, forgiving each other, just as in Christ God forgave you."* - Ephesians 4:32

Reflection: As Black women, we may struggle with forgiveness due to past experiences of injustice and hurt. However, as believers in Christ, we are reminded to practice forgiveness, just as God has forgiven us through the sacrifice of Jesus.

The Bible verse for today reminds us that we should be kind, compassionate, and forgiving towards others, as God has been towards us. We need to understand that forgiveness is not just for the benefit of the person we are forgiving, but also for our own emotional and spiritual well-being.

Practice: Take some time today to reflect on the people and situations that you need to forgive. Make a plan to practice forgiveness, whether it be through writing a letter of forgiveness (even if you don't send it), praying for the person or situation, or seeking guidance from a therapist or spiritual advisor.

Prayer: Dear Lord, we come to you today to acknowledge the struggles we face in understanding and practicing forgiveness. We ask for your guidance and strength as we work to forgive those who have hurt us. We trust in your forgiveness toward us and strive to embody that forgiveness toward others. Amen.

Affirmation: I understand and practice forgiveness, as God has forgiven me through the sacrifice of Jesus.

Day 28: Cultivating inner peace and tranquility

Bible Verse: *"Peace I leave with you; my peace I give you. I do not give to you as the world gives. Do not let your hearts be troubled and do not be afraid."* - John 14:27

Reflection: As Black women, we may struggle with cultivating inner peace and tranquility due to societal pressures and stress. However, as believers in Christ, we are reminded that the peace that Jesus gives us is not like the world gives. He offers a peace that surpasses all understanding and can guard our hearts and minds.

The Bible verse for today reminds us that Jesus gives us peace, and we should not let our hearts be troubled or afraid. We need to seek inner peace and tranquility through our relationship with God, by connecting with Him through prayer, reading His word, and listening to His guidance.

Practice: Take some time today to reflect on what causes stress and anxiety in your life. Make a plan to cultivate inner peace and tranquility, whether it be through daily quiet time with God, practicing mindfulness, or engaging in calming activities such as yoga or meditation.

Prayer: Dear Lord, we come to you today acknowledging the struggles we face in cultivating inner peace and tranquility. We ask for your guidance and help in seeking inner peace and tranquility through our relationship with you. We trust in your promise to give us peace and we surrender our hearts and minds to you. Amen.

Affirmation: I cultivate inner peace and tranquility by seeking it through my relationship with God and by surrendering my heart and mind to him.

Day 29: Reflecting on personal growth and progress

Bible Verse: *"But grow in the grace and knowledge of our Lord and Savior Jesus Christ. To him be the glory both now and forever. Amen."* - 2 Peter 3:18

Reflection: As Black women, we may struggle with feeling like we haven't made progress or grown in certain areas of our lives. However, as believers in Christ, we are reminded to continually grow in grace and knowledge of Jesus and that this growth is not a one-time event but a lifelong process.

The Bible verse for today reminds us that we should continually grow in grace and knowledge of Jesus Christ. We need to reflect on our personal growth and progress, celebrate our accomplishments, and identify areas where we need to continue to grow.

Practice: Take some time today to reflect on your personal growth and progress over the past year. Make a list of accomplishments and areas where you have grown. Identify areas where you would like to continue to grow in the coming year, whether it be in your faith, personal relationships, career, or other areas.

Prayer: Dear Lord, we come to you today to acknowledge the struggles we face in reflecting on personal growth and progress. We ask for your guidance and help in celebrating our accomplishments and identifying areas where we need to continue to grow. We trust in your promise to help us grow in grace and knowledge of you. Amen.

Affirmation: I reflect on my personal growth and progress and celebrate my accomplishments while identifying areas where I need to continue to grow, with the help of Jesus.

Day 30: Embracing Hope and Looking Forward to the Future

Bible Verse: *"For I know the plans I have for you, declares the Lord, plans to prosper you and not to harm you, plans to give you hope and a future."* - Jeremiah 29:11

Reflection: As Black women, we may struggle with embracing hope and looking forward to the future due to systemic issues and racism. However, as believers in Christ, we are reminded that God has plans for us to prosper and give us hope and a future.

The Bible verse for today reminds us that God has plans for us and that He wants to give us hope and a future. It's important for us to trust in God's plan for our lives and to embrace hope for the future, knowing that He is in control and will always be with us.

Practice: Take some time today to reflect on your hopes and dreams for the future. Make a plan to work towards those hopes and dreams, whether it be through setting goals, seeking guidance or support, and reminding yourself of God's plan and presence in your life.

Prayer: Dear Lord, we come to you today acknowledging the struggles we face in embracing hope and looking forward to the future. We ask for your guidance and strength as we work toward our hopes and dreams. We trust in your promise to prosper us and give us hope and a future. Amen.

Affirmation: I trust in God's plan for my life and embrace hope for the future, knowing that He is in control and will always be with me.

III. Additional Resources

Books: There are many books available that offer guidance and inspiration for Black women on their faith journey. Some recommended titles include "The Purpose of Woman" by Taffi Dollar, "Becoming a Woman of Grace" by Cynthia Heald, and "A Black Woman's Guide to Church" by Kimberley Kennedy.

Online Communities: There are several online communities and forums available that provide a space for Black women to connect and discuss their faith journey. Some examples include "Sisters in Christ" on Facebook, "Black Christian Women" on Instagram, and "The Sister Circle" on Twitter.

Podcasts: Podcasts can be a great way to stay informed and inspired on your faith journey. Some recommended podcasts for Black women include "The Sister Circle", "The Kingdom Driven Entrepreneur", and "The Bible for Normal People"

Counseling and Therapy: It is important to seek help and guidance if you are struggling with mental and emotional well-being. Christian counseling and therapy can provide a safe space to discuss and work through any issues related to your faith and how it affects your life.

Bible Study Groups: Joining a Bible study group can provide a supportive and encouraging environment for growth and learning. It can also be a great way to connect with other Black women who share your faith.

Local Church: Joining a local church can provide a sense of community and support as well as opportunities for worship, fellowship, and service. It can also provide opportunities for mentorship and spiritual guidance.

Remember that it is important to find what works best for you in terms of additional resources and support. Don't be afraid to reach out and seek help when you need it. The most important thing is that you continue to grow in your faith and relationship with God.

IV. Conclusion

As we come to the end of this 30-day devotional, it is important to take a moment to reflect on the past month and the progress we have made in our faith journey. We have explored themes such as resilience, self-care, trust in God's plan, cultural heritage, community building, personal growth, and more. These themes have provided guidance and inspiration for us to continue to grow and strengthen our relationship with God.

It is important to remember that this is just the beginning and our faith journey is a lifelong process. As we continue to navigate our daily lives, it is important to seek guidance and support in our faith journey. This can be done through reading and studying the Bible, connecting with a community of believers, seeking guidance from a mentor or spiritual advisor, and finding additional resources that resonate with us.

We encourage you to continue to reflect on the themes and practices we have covered in this devotional and to make them a part of your daily life. Remember, you are not alone in this journey, and with faith and determination, you can continue to grow in your relationship with God.

Made in the USA
Monee, IL
16 June 2023

35956770R00033